POSITIVE AFFIRMATIONS FOR BLACK WOMEN

POWERFUL AFFIRMATIONS TO GET BACK YOUR POWER AND LIVE FULLY

DEBORAH FREEMAN

CONTENTS

COPYRIGHT

All rights reserved. No part of this publication may be reproduced, distributed, or transmitted in any form or by any means, including photocopying, recording, or any electronic or mechanical methods, without the prior written permission of the publisher except in the case of brief quotations embodied in critical reviews and certain other non-commercial uses permitted by copyright law.

INTRODUCTION

Phrases have power and positive affirmations are a means of employing particular words to transform your thinking patterns and bring power, energy, love, compassion, and a whole host of other light components to your inner voice. Simply stating your positive affirmations aloud every day has been proven to increase your mental health but if the concept of saying them aloud is too frightening, you can either write them down or utilize them in meditation practice as a mantra.

Using positive affirmations as a regular practice is vital since the main aim is to materialize these thoughts into reality. Our internal voice may be harsh, judgmental, and excessively critical and by recognizing yourself when your inner mean girl is ruling the roost you can start to become more conscious of which positive affirmations you may need to embrace. Perhaps your inner cruel girl is continuously knocking your looks down or reminding you that you are a bad decision-maker. It's time to alter that narrative. By speaking words of love repeatedly every single day you will come to own that story and this will reflect in how you navigate around the world.

WHAT ARE AFFIRMATIONS?

Affirmations are merely the action or process of affirming something or being affirmed

An affirmation is generally a phrase, a sentence of strong words put together, like a positive statement, and this sentence is designed to tap into your conscious and unconscious mind to encourage you, challenge you, and push you to attain your full potential in life.

Affirmations are a self-help approach used to increase self-confidence and conviction in your skills.

WHY ARE AFFIRMATIONS IMPORTANT?

The advantages of Affirmations are infinite, they have helped a plethora of individuals all around the globe accomplish great things, but more significantly, they may help you make good changes in your life.

Affirmations have the power to motivate you to act on certain thoughts, help you to focus on achieving your goals in life, give you the power to change your negative patterns of thought and replace them with positive patterns of thought, assist you in adopting a new belief system, but most of all, affirmations can re-establish the positivity back into your life and help regain as well as increase your self-confidence.

Affirmations may assist build good energy around your life, money, and finances, ending the negative cycle of anxiety and tension. By moving your energy to a more positive level, you may feel better about your finances and possibilities, starting to materialize the riches and money you seek.

In addition, affirmations change you into the development mentality that attracts riches and chances.

WILL THEY WORK FOR ME?

Yes! It is scientifically established. The practice and popularity of positive affirmations are based on well-acknowledged and well-established psychological theories.

First, let's discuss Neuroplasticity. Your brain has a tremendous capacity to alter and adapt to diverse conditions throughout your life. How you utilize your brain will modify your brain. Thinking patterns - both good and negative - will run specific "train tracks" into your brain. The longer you utilize the same track, the deeper, more automatic, and easier it becomes. So what you practice, you become. And that's why and how affirmations work. They will establish "positive railway tracks" and change the bad ones.

According to positivepsychology.com "affirmations are aimed to create an optimistic outlook. And optimism in itself is a strong thing. In terms of lowering negative thoughts, affirmations have been demonstrated to assist with the propensity to dwell on unfavorable events.

When we can cope with negative messages and replace them with positive claims, we may develop more adaptable, optimistic narratives about who we are and what we can achieve.

HOW TO PRACTICE DAILY AFFIRMATIONS

To obtain the maximum advantage from affirmations, you'll want to start a regular practice and make it a habit, that's something that all the various sources can agree upon. How frequently and how precisely is far more up to discussion and varying viewpoints.

Here's a roundup of typical advice:

Start with 3 to 5 minutes at least twice a day. Upon waking up and going into bed, for example. Or while you're putting on your makeup or shaving so that you may look at yourself in the mirror as you repeat the positive sentence. Using an existing habit or action as a trigger makes it much simpler to create a new habit.

Repeat each affirmation roughly 10 times. Listen to yourself saying it, believing it to be real. "Breathe" into the affirmation as you are saying it. You want to go beyond the notion of the affirmation to an actual, positive expression of the trait you want.

Ask a trustworthy loved one or a coach to assist. Listening to someone else repeat your affirmations may assist reaffirm your conviction in them.

Combine it with other positive thinking and goal-setting tools. For instance, affirmations work especially well with visualization, helping you lend more life and vividness to what you're saying. Bold Tuesday's Vision Board Reimagined gives a terrific approach to include affirmation cards into your vision board, so you can connect the two disciplines.

Be patient. It may take some time before you see any results, so stay with your practice!

AFFIRMATIONS FOR CONFIDENCE

I have power, happiness, health, and self-assurance.

Everything I want in life is mine to have.

I have complete affection for myself.

I am capable, shrewd, and competent.

I'm improving as I mature and change.

I adore the person I'm becoming.

I am evolving into a better version of myself every day.

It's wonderful to be alive today!

I am a person of strength and force.

I have a natural sense of comfort and confidence in my own life.

I am admirable, intelligent, and deserving.

I make decisions for myself with clarity and confidence.

I have natural confidence.

My whole being is strong and profound—body, mind, and soul.

My confidence is increasing every day.

I have a strong sense of motivation, optimism, and self-assurance.

I have entire faith in who I am and what I'm doing.

I have faith in my abilities and talents.

I exude love and self-assurance.

Though modest, I am certain.

I have faith in my future while living in the amazing moment that is now.

I approach difficult circumstances with conviction, bravery, and confidence.

I am glad to share my special abilities and endowments with the world since I am self-assured in them.

I am resourceful, tough, and self-sufficient.

My issues all have solutions.

Nobody is better than myself.

I am a confident person.

I have faith that I can transform my life.

My life is peaceful right now.

Every day and in every aspect, I'm growing better.

I experience wonderful things every day.

I have all I need to make today fantastic.

I exude assurance.

I am sufficient.

I overcome every challenge to build the life of my dreams.

Everything is proceeding as expected.

My future won't be shaped by the past.

My ideal world is one that I have created.

I constantly look for the positive in others and in myself.

I am confident in my capacity to carry out my life's objectives.

I have faith in my life plan and the course of events.

I am given the affection I deserve.

I embrace all that is positive in myself and let go of my negative self-perceptions.

I sense a wonderful, vibrant energy. I am awake and moving.

I am surrounded by plenty.

My experiences are crucial to my development and evolution.

I respect who I am, thus I am worthy.

I'm up for fresh, lovely changes.

I'm having wonderful experiences thanks to life.

Nobody except myself determines my emotions.

I control my ideas, and I will make an accurate assessment of myself.

AFFIRMATIONS FOR SUCCESS

Life is going well for me.

I am certain that I can fulfill any life goal.

Wealth comes to me and flows through me.

By attracting those who can assist me, I will be successful.

I am aware that a good outlook may help me succeed.

I have a lot of energy. My greatest advantages for moving me closer to achievement are my self-belief, optimism, and confidence.

I'm content with who I am and what I can do.

I'm going to say goodbye to my old bad habits today and say hello to a great transformation in my life.

I have the ability to pursue my goals and make my ambitions a reality.

I am prepared for today. I'm ready for success, adoration, joy, serenity, and wealth! I'm ready for my most improbable aspirations to come true.

I am the one who designs my future. I can fulfill my own personal goals.

I can overcome any obstacle and hardship that stands in my path.

I am fortunate to have all I need to have a successful life.

I have the power to draw everyday abundance.

I am aware of success's richness.

I am grateful for what I have in abundance.

I have faith in myself.

I am receptive to unforeseen chances.

I make the decision to accept life's enigma.

My greatest source of inspiration is myself.

I have the capacity to excel.

I am appreciative of the riches I now enjoy and that is on the horizon.

Miracles find their way into my life.

I succeed in whatever I put my mind to.

I am open to all potential outcomes.

There are no ceilings to what I can do as I continue to go higher.

I am a powerful person who draws pleasure and prosperity to myself.

I let go of ingrained, unfavorable notions that had prevented me from succeeding.

My light is needed in the world, and I am not scared to shine.

I gain self-assurance, strength, and success every day.

I deserve every wonderful thing life has to give, even success.

I am constantly willing to consider new approaches to achievement.

I am a strong maker. I design and live the life I desire.

I am surrounded by optimistic, encouraging individuals who have faith in me.

I am passionate about what I do every day and maintain focus on my objective.

I'm proud of my capacity to leave a positive mark on the planet.

I can see wealth wherever I turn.

More doors open for me as I let more abundance into my life.

Money keeps coming into my life.

My activities continuously produce money, success, and plenty.

I am completely abundant in my life right now.

I think I'm capable of anything.

I intend to realize my aspirations and ambitions.

I am a goal-setter who will do whatever to accomplish my objectives.

I'm dedicated to succeeding in every aspect of my life.

I choose optimism.

I'm building the career of my dreams and deserving of the position I want.

I have faith in myself.

I effortlessly achieve all of my objectives.

I am sufficient.

AFFIRMATIONS FOR ABUNDANCE

I draw money.

Money is never an issue for me.

I am appreciative of money.

Everyone has access to enough money, in my opinion.

With my money, I am kind.

Financial freedom is mine.

I get through my financial challenges.

I get a surprise payment.

I reach my financial objectives.

I am surrounded by energy that is abundant.

I am able to easily make money.

I attract money to myself.

Money loves me, and I adore money.

I take advantage of all available cash chances.

I have an attitude of abundance.

I have a prosperous life.

I have enough.

Each day, I draw prosperity to myself.

My life is flooded with money.

Opportunities for fortune abound in my life.

I was made for plenty.

Today will be a successful day.

I keep attracting plenty.

For me, plenty comes naturally.

I have much more than I need.

I see chances for financial success everywhere.

My earnings are always rising.

I am open to all potential outcomes.

I'll take payment in any manner.

I am able to achieve money and success.

I deserve to be wealthy.

I use my wealth to impact the world.

I let go of all opposition to drawing money.

I freely distribute the money I am given.

The cosmos is abundant, and I have no trouble connecting to it.

I am blessed with nature.

I am capable of living a prosperous life.

I already have money.

I am a good money manager.

I am conscious of riches everywhere.

I excel at generating income.

I have enough money to cover all of my goals and requirements.

I'm improving my financial situation.

My bank accounts are growing in value.

I have the ability and desire to produce money.

I think of innovative methods to raise my revenue.

I deserve to be paid for my work.

I contribute to the world and get paid for it.

Everything I need is always available.

My money are within my control.

I have faith that I can generate plenty.

I have a stable income.

Money Making is simple and enjoyable.

I already have everything I need to achieve my financial goals.

I'm wealthy beyond measure.

I have a happy and prosperous life.

My financial situation is precisely as it should be.

My abundant ideas result in a rich existence.

I have the capacity to flourish.

I am appreciative of whatever I have and get.

I have money and prosperity in my life.

I constantly generate business possibilities.

I have unlimited financial possibilities in the future.

I am an efficient money maker.

All the riches I want are continuously given to me by the cosmos.

My financial options are limitless.

My money is in my hands.

I'll succeed in all of my financial objectives.

Every day, my finances go better.

I don't have an issue with money.

I am self-sufficient financially.

I do not depend on anybody for my financial needs.

I have enough money to fulfill all of my needs.

I have money.

I use my financial potential today.

My wealth increases daily.

Money is never a concern for me.

I'm drawn to money.

My talents and abilities are continually being converted into riches and earnings.

I'm deserving of and expecting much.

My path to new financial prospects is about to open.

I make money doing what I like most.

Everything I want in terms of plenty is already on its way to me.

My life keeps becoming more and more financially.

From and to me, plenty flows in all ways.

I have a prosperous life.

My fortune continuously helps me and the people I care about.

I choose wisely financially.

I have good financial sense.

I make it a point to daily follow the road of plenty.

I consistently make choices that improve my financial situation.

The universe's abundance is moving in my direction.

My financial issues are easily resolved.

I am unable to be denied the prosperity and abundance I deserve.

AFFIRMATIONS FOR HEALTH

With each deep breath, my body is becoming better.

My physique is fit and powerful.

My body is strong and capable of self-healing.

My health and body are renewed by my optimistic ideas and deeds.

I have a right to feel strong and alive.

Taking care of myself feels amazing.

My body is capable of astounding feats.

Everything is constantly going my way.

I treat my body well.

My birthright is to give my body a rest.

I will treat my body with respect because it is holy.

To respect the power of my body, I workout.

I treat my body well.

My physique is ideal in its current state.
I am joyful, optimistic, and in good health.

I'm appreciative of my life energy.

My robust immune system keeps me protected.

I believe my body can tell me what it needs, therefore I pay attention.

I eat to satisfy my body's needs and to honor it.

I have a good night's rest.

Always working for me is my physique.

My body is not here for other people.

My intellect is a strong instrument.

I find it simple to adore myself.

I crave new activities and encounters.

I deserve to be well.

I give my body the respect and care that it deserves.

My body is an energy of peace.

I don't carry any strain or stress in my body.

I adore and accept myself.

I have a right to be confident.

I should have a long and healthy life.

I work out to demonstrate my love for my body.

I go through life incrementally.

I'm entitled to occupy this area.

I am loving, witty, and brilliant.

I'm bursting with fortitude.

I am proud of who I am.

Anything I put my mind to, I can achieve.

I am important.

I am thankful for the past, present, and future.

I'll take care of myself.

I deserve the very best.

I let go of anxiety and dread.

I am strong.

The situation is OK.

I am living in the now.

I am in charge of my own thinking.

I'm a part of nature.

I'm secure.

In freedom.

From the inside out, I shine.

I feel revived and energized when I awake.

I have an amazing body.

I let tranquility pass through me.

I have access to all feelings whenever I choose.

Better than perfect is done.

My body feels energized.

I feel well in body, mind, and soul.

Relationship confirmations

I'm determined to improve my connection.

I am in control of my own happiness.

I'm deserving of love.

I'm willing to accept love.

I'm determined to be a nice, loving person in my relationship.

I'm surrounded with love.

I'm allowed to request what I need from my relationship.

I am worthy of love simply the way I am.

I let my spouse have their own identity.

In my relationship, I relinquish power.

I go into my relationship with a heart open.

I have confidence in our connection.

I provide the time and consideration it requires to my connection.

I am really likable.

I create room in my life for a wonderful relationship.

I think there is unending love.

I deserve to be content in my relationship.

All of the connections in my life are appreciated by me.

I give my relationship my whole self.

I let go of anger toward my spouse and make a loving request for what I need.

I promise to establish appropriate limits in my relationship.

I respect the limits set by my spouse.

I'm accountable for my own feelings.

Every day, I express my thanks to my companion.

I give my girlfriend and I time to be together.

I have compassion and affection for my lover.

I provide my partner an unbiased and heartfelt ear.

I am certain that I will be OK no matter what occurs in my relationship.

I am overflowing with compassion.

I consistently work to be the greatest version of myself in my relationship.

I'm going to do something kind for my spouse today.

I am capable of having wholesome, productive conversations.

I like our contrasts because they keep things fascinating and new in our relationship.

I promise to be a devoted, encouraging companion.

In this connection, my wants are significant and legitimate.

Deep love and respect should be shown to both my spouse and I.

Everything about my spouse is wonderful.

I am grateful for all my spouse does to support our union.

I have faith in our union.

I inject flirting and humor into our connection.

It's acceptable that I don't always get things perfect.

Every day I give my relationship my best.

AFFIRMATIONS FOR LOVE

My person's list of priorities starts with me.

On my list of priorities, my person is at the top.

My partner loves me very much.

My partner is appreciative of having me in their life.

Being yourself with my person allows me to feel completely at ease.

The more I love someone, the more they will love me back.

My partner becomes more in love with me every day.

When my person sees me, their eyes sparkle.

My relationship with my partner is unique and distinctive.

The connection between us deepens daily.

I'm prepared for a fulfilling partnership with this individual.

My partner is prepared to adore me without conditions.

I am loved and cherished by my special someone for who I am on the inside.

my partner solely has eyes for me.

My person feels pulled to me more and more each day.

I want to spend the rest of my life with this individual.

The affection that unites the two of us is strong.

I feel at peace with the world when I'm with this individual.

With me, my partner feels secure.

Around me, my partner feels free to be who they are.

My special someone accepts and loves me despite all of my imperfections.

My person has made the decision to love me despite the circumstances.

I'm the first person this individual calls when they're feeling depressed.

I have a lot of similarities with my person.

They look around a busy room for me.

This individual and I are connected by heavenly love.

My partner holds me in the highest regard.

I have the utmost regard for this individual.

There has been a connection between us ever since we first met.

We shall always be together, no matter where life takes us.

Every time we are together, everything is perfect.

Calling my partner is usually a quick and easy process.

My partner gives me their confidence and trust.

When I'm not around, my person thinks about me.

my partner thinks about me while they are listening to a love song.

I allow my particular individual to love and care for me with an open heart.

I welcome this individual into my life.

My partner finds it impossible to imagine their existence without me.

Simply by being myself, I am drawing this individual to me at all times.

This individual and I are being brought together by the universe.

I meet every need this individual has for a mate.

Everything I could possibly want in a life mate is in my person.

Our personalities blend well together and complement one another.

I want to spend my whole life with this guy.

My person is drawn to me inexorably when they glance at me.

My partner feels a strong spiritual connection with me.

My partner helps me achieve my goals.

This individual believes that I am behind them in all they want to do.

My companion feels comfortable telling me anything.

I'm drawing people who really connect with me.

This individual believes in our shared future.

My partner finds it impossible to picture life without me.

I'll be in a contented partnership with this individual.

I can be open and transparent with my partner.

I am certain that my special someone will stand by my side no matter what.

I have faith that the universe is conspiring to connect me and this individual.

I create a place in my life for my soul partner.

The Universe wishes to provide me with a happy, healthy relationship.

When they see me, my partner experiences intense desire.

My encounter with them makes them feel fortunate.

My partner believes they can put all of their faith in me.

This person's life path precisely complements mine.

I have faith that the proper love will find me.

I have faith that the love I have for my partner will be reciprocated.

My partner and I will have an exquisite connection.

We both put a lot of effort into our connection.

AFFIRMATIONS FOR BUSINESS

I adore what I do.

I like having a positive approach.

I'm appreciative of all the qualities I have that make me successful.

I am appreciative of the money my company has brought me.

I am grateful for any chance that comes my way.

I'm ready for another successful day of productivity.

Today, I am attracting fantastic business prospects.

Today promises to be a fruitful day full of chances and ideas.
Nothing or anybody can prevent me from achieving my objectives today.

Today, I intentionally choose to be joyful and upbeat.

I am quite certain that I can succeed.

I have the endurance to endure adversity.

I can listen well.

My enterprise is advantageous to myself and society.

I have the ideal business strategy.

I am a master at whatever I do.

I will stop at nothing to see that my company succeeds.

The difficulties I encounter in my work keep me inspired and motivated.

I am using my company to fulfill my goal in life.

I give thanks to the universe for my exceptional abilities and charitable outlook.

I am happy with my life's achievements.

Every day, I open doors for progress for both myself and others.

I seek advice and inspiration from my peers.

My basic principles are in line with my business goal.

I am competent to manage my company.

I am capable of doing anything.

I have faith that my company will succeed.

I'm quite savvy in business.

I run a prosperous company.

I'm having an impact on the globe.

I am a top-tier businesswoman.

I'm doing better today than I did yesterday.

I get stronger as a result of the difficulties and obstacles I face.

The finest company in the world is mine.

I get better every day.

For me, nothing is insurmountable.

Every day, my confidence increases.

I'm excellent at solving problems.

Every time, I am in the ideal situation.

I control my destiny and am the captain of my soul.

I like the independence and flexibility that my company gives me.

I can live the life I desire because of my business.

I own a thriving company that I am enthusiastic about.

I can make rapid judgments since my thinking is concentrated and clear.

I am really good at managing my time.

I make wise selections and am steadfast and uncompromising.

I learn from my errors and don't commit them again.

I have faith in myself.

I have faith in my skills.

I was destined to launch my own business.

Every day, I work to establish a profitable business.

I am motivated by purpose and enthusiasm.

My company is expanding just as I had hoped.

My activities and thoughts are focused on expanding my company.

My partners and colleagues put forth a lot of effort and are encouraging.

Offering my fellow humans employment opportunities makes me happy and fulfilled.

In my workforce, I draw in individuals that are joyful, energized, and productive.

I'm grateful to be surrounded by accomplished and encouraging individuals.

I am fortunate to work with folks that are passionate and energized.

I am skilled at assigning tasks to increase productivity.

I appreciate the time and effort my employees have put in.

I am a fantastic employer because I have a strong sense of loyalty to my staff.

I have a fantastic team working with me to grow my company.

My hardworking staff significantly increases the worth of my company.

I pay attention to my coworkers' criticism and suggestions, and I use both in my professional and personal life.

I get along well with my coworkers.

I woo the greatest people to work with me.

My team members adore me because of my contagious optimism and energy.

My company's success is entirely up to me. I'm the one who has to pay.

I firmly think that successful businesses are built on happy customers and content staff.

I naturally take the lead.

To operate the company, I have a fantastic team of motivated and accomplished people.

I am surrounded by individuals that love, respect and support me without condition.

My staff looks to me for leadership and counsel.

Customers truly desire what I'm delivering.

I am giving my clients genuine value.

My customers like working with me because I have a fantastic sense of humor.

I'm in the business of making my customers happy.

My upbeat demeanor draws the proper type of customers.

Interacting with my clientele is fun for me.

I can quickly win over devoted clients with my excitement and drive.

Customers that work with me have better lives.

My customers like my dependability and commitment to finishing tasks on schedule.

I'm concerned about my customers' fulfillment and happiness.

I just consider the advantages for clients while making business choices.

I think a successful business depends on happy customers.

Customers get value from my company.

Every day, I get new, devoted clients.

My customers are ready and thrilled to work with me.

I am capable of realizing my professional objectives.

I'm coming closer to achieving my business goals every day.

I am confidently making progress toward my objectives.

My company is doing well, just as I had hoped.

I always go above and beyond what is required of me to complete the task.

I'm letting go of worries and skepticism about achieving the objective.

I always accomplish my objectives on schedule.

I like pursuing goals and achieving them every time.

I like setting objectives and working toward them according to a plan.

I am capable of achieving everything I set my mind to in life since I am intelligent and persistent.

I use challenges as a chance to further my objectives.

I make a sincere effort to accomplish my objectives.

I confidently go in the direction of my objectives.

All of the daily objectives I set for myself are always met.

For me, achieving challenging objectives is a piece of cake.

I keep making progress toward my objective.

I'll easily get past obstacles and challenges to accomplish my aim.

I make the appropriate judgments swiftly to accomplish my objectives.

My choices are consistent with my objectives.

I'm motivated and excited as I strive to accomplish new objectives.

I promote my goods and services easily because I am confident in them.

Working smarter leads to more productivity, and I live by this guideline.

Every day I'm breaking sales records.

Opportunities abound for my company.

My company is doing well, just as I had hoped.

I'm recording fresh sales every day.

My business's marketing comes easy to me.

I keep getting fresh offers.

I am a master at selling my goods and services.

I am excellent at managing businesses.

My goods and services are always becoming better.

I am open to fresh suggestions and chances to grow my company.

I have mad marketing skills.

I provide the finest goods and services available.

I don't skimp on the quality of the goods or services I provide.

My everyday investment in my career and my company is paying off handsomely.

My company receives money easily.

Every dollar I put into my company multiplies back to me.

My company's financial status is solid and secure.

I have faith in my abilities to generate income.

I've thrown wide the doors to abundant money.

I'm content and at peace when I'm financially secure.

My skill and diligence have brought me success.

Every month, my income increases significantly.

I invest the cash I've worked so hard to obtain back into my company.

To increase the profit margin, I know when to take prudent risks.

My business choices are made to enhance my company's chances.

I earn enough money to support my family and myself.

To manage my company, I always have more than enough money.

I have so many business-generating ideas.

I attract success like a magnet.

I'm worthy of success.

My company is successful because of my love for what I do.

My capacity for change-taking aids my professional success.

I'm inherently successful.

My efforts and ideas help me achieve the success I hope for.

In everything I encounter, I see a chance.

I succeed with ease.

I already possess every element necessary for success.

I value and respect my accomplishments.

I don't readily give up. My tenacity pays off in achievement.

I will succeed because I am meant to.

On the right track to success, I am.

My company has had great success.

My company is growing every day.

I'm prepared to experience the success I deserve.

More success follows each triumph.

By doing what I love and enjoy, my wealth is increasing every day.

My company is about to see rapid expansion.
I'm committed to doing well in business.

AFFIRMATIONS FOR MONEY

I have an attitude of abundance.

I'm enjoying an abundant existence.

I have enough.

I'm appreciative of everything in my life.

I am grateful for all the joy each day provides me.

I attract money and plenty every day.

Riches come into and go out of my life constantly.

I freely give away the riches I am given.

The ability to produce riches and plenty is all around us in life.

I'm willing to bring prosperity to myself.

I deserve the richness that often enters my life.

I am appreciative of my life's prosperity and riches.

Any chance that comes my way, I will take.

I have the correct frame of mind to draw riches into my life.

I was made for plenty.

I shall be successful today and attract plenty into my life.

I'm willing to make my life abundant.

In this cosmos, there is an infinite amount of plenty, and I will use my ability to access it.

Positive emotions and feelings of well-being attract a tremendous quantity of riches.

I'm accustomed to feeling wealthy.

I'm good at seeing the bright side.

I gratefully cover my expenditures.

I have much more than I need.

I'm kind with the money I have.

I can see opportunities everywhere.

I have no trouble getting money, both expected and unanticipated.

I am delighted by others' successes and am motivated by them.

My earnings are always rising.

Everyone, including myself, has more than enough.

I'm blessed by nature.

In my life, there is always sufficient.

Financial freedom is mine.

I attract prosperity and good fortune like a magnet.

I am generous.